Cesar Chavez
lived from
1927 to 1993.

Cesar Chavez spent more than 40 years helping farmworkers have a better life. Keep reading to learn about this leader who fought for change.

When he was young, Cesar liked to play with his brothers, sisters, and cousins.

Cesar was born in Arizona in 1927. His grandparents had come to the United States from Mexico years before. Cesar and his family lived on their farm.

Cesar's family was sad to leave their home.

In the 1930s, there was very little rain in Arizona. The land dried up and farmers couldn't grow **crops**. Cesar's family had to move. They went west to California.

Many of the migrant farmworkers were Mexican-American, like Cesar's family.

California had a lot of farmland. Cesar's family got jobs as **migrant farmworkers**. That meant they moved from farm to farm to pick crops. It was hard work, and the pay was very low.

Cesar worked in the fields to help his family. He also went to school. He liked to learn, but he didn't like going to school. Some kids and teachers made fun of him because he did not speak English well.

Cesar and Helen's first child was a boy named Fernando.

When Cesar was 17, he joined the navy. He was at sea for two years. After he returned home, he married his true love, Helen Fabela. They later had eight children.

Even when it was hot, the landowners wouldn't let the workers rest.

Cesar returned to working in the fields. But he was angry about how hard life was for the farmworkers. The landowners made all the money. They didn't treat the workers well.

These were some of the ways in which life was difficult for migrant farmworkers:

* They made very little money.

* They worked long hours each day.

* They were not given clean water to drink while they worked.

* They were not allowed to rest during the day.

* At night they had to stay in small shacks with dirt floors.

Cesar had always been quiet and shy. But now he decided it was time to speak up. He was going to work for farmworkers' rights.

Cesar told farmworkers that it was important to vote.

He began by talking to farmworkers.
He helped them **register** to vote.
If they voted, they could help choose
America's leaders.

The eagle on this sign stood for the farmworkers' union.

FARM WORKERS ASSOCIATION

Cesar also got thousands of farm-workers to join a **union**, or workers' group. He said that if the workers joined together, the landowners would have to listen to them.

In 1965, some California grape pickers were being paid even less than other grape pickers. Cesar led the workers on a **strike**. This meant that they would not work until the landowners agreed to pay them more.

He also planned a **boycott**. He asked people to stop buying grapes from farms that treated workers unfairly.

The farmworkers carried flags and signs as they marched.

Later he led a march to Sacramento, the capital city of California. Cesar and other farmworkers walked more than 300 miles. Their feet hurt badly, but they kept going.

In Sacramento, Cesar told the marchers they had won.

All their hard work had paid off. The California landowners finally agreed to pay the workers more money. Cesar and the union had won! But there was more work to do.

Cesar showed that people can make a difference by working together.

Cesar spent the rest of his life helping farmworkers. He died in 1993. But people will never forget the man who said "Sí, se puede." This means, "Yes, it can be done."

Glossary

boycott (noun) a group's refusal to deal with a business or person, in order to bring about change

crop (noun) a plant grown in large amounts, often for food

migrant farmworker (noun) a person who travels from one farm to another to find work

register (verb) to sign up

strike (noun) a group's refusal to work, in order to have changes made

union (noun) an organization of workers formed to protect the rights of its members